Life, Death and Life after Death

by Karl Lawson

Series Editor: Roger J. Owen

Note about dates

This book uses the abbreviations CE and BCE for Common Era and Before the Common Era. In some books you will find AD (Anno Domini) for CE and BC (Before Christ) for BCE. The actual years are the same, only the tag is different.

Credits

The author and publishers are grateful to the following for permission to reproduce copyright photographs in this book:

Science/Society Picture Library: p.8; Derek Goodwin: P.10; Andy Weber: p.26; Corbis: p.29, p.30; World Religions: p.17 (bottom), p.18, p.20, p.27; Arthur Baker: p.35

Every effort has been made to contact copyright holders of material reproduced in this publication. Any omission will be rectified in subsequent printings if notice is given to the publisher. While the information in this publication is believed to be true and accurate at the date of going to press, neither the author nor the publisher can accept any legal responsibility for any errors or omissions that may be made.

Roger J. Owen, Series Editor

Roger J. Owen was Head of RE in a variety of schools for thirty years, as well as being a Head of Faculty, advisory teacher for primary and secondary RE, Section 23 Inspector and 'O' Level and GCSE Chief Examiner. Author of seventeen educational titles, he is currently an education consultant and WJEC Religious Studies AS and A2 Chair of Examiners.

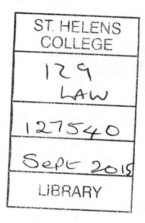
Published by UWIC Press
UWIC, Cyncoed Road,
Cardiff CF23 6XD
cgrove@uwic.ac.uk
029 2041 6515

ISBN 978-1-905617-13-5

Design by the info group
Picture research by Glyn Saunders Jones
Printed by MWL Digital

Sponsored by the Welsh Assembly Government
© 2006 Karl Lawson

Cover: Mystique of the Supreme (World Religions)

Life, Death and Life after Death

by Karl Lawson
Series Editor: Roger J. Owen

Contents

Chapter 1

Tackling the Topic

Life, Death and Life after Death is an interesting and challenging area to study, as it raises fundamental issues about human existence. It involves consideration of the nature and purpose (if any) of human life. It investigates the evidence for existence beyond the grave. It examines the impact of belief in life after death on the behaviour of believers and their attitudes to death.

That the study of Life, Death and Life after Death is a crucial part of your A Level course is evident from the fact that 40% of A2 marks, 20% of the entire A Level, are allocated to it. Indeed, from 2010 onwards it will be allocated 50% of the A2 marks and 25% of the entire A level. It is a unique part of your course because it is only through this theme that you demonstrate your skills in linking different areas of Religious Studies.

What you need to do

To achieve the highest grade in the synoptic assessment you need to demonstrate:
- knowledge and understanding of the issues involved in attitudes to, and concepts of life, death and life after death in at least two distinct areas (e.g. Judaism and Islam);
- knowledge and understanding of the connections between relevant elements of these areas;
- ability to relate these areas to a relevant aspect of human experience (e.g. the need to face death);
- ability to make relevant comparisons and contrasts between these areas;
- appropriate use of technical language and terminology;
- knowledge, understanding and analysis of relevant views of scholars and/or schools of thought;
- ability to support arguments with appropriate examples from these areas;
- ability to evaluate different points of view and reach an appropriate conclusion;
- high quality of language, including clarity in expression and coherence in structure.

N.B. From 2010, synopticity is required in all A2 modules and may be demonstrated by exploring connections between elements of a single area of study, not necessarily two or more areas. Therefore, comments in this chapter about two or more areas may be ignored after 2009.

What help to expect

You can expect a reasonable amount of guidance from your teacher. Indeed, usually the role of the teacher is vital to student success. Teachers want you to do well and are there to teach relevant topics and stimulate interest in them.

Your teacher should:
- tell you about the pre-examination information and advise you what key aspects of the theme to concentrate on (e.g. it is unwise to concentrate on life after death if the focus of the question is the nature and purpose of human life);

- make you aware of the assessment demands of the level descriptors, the basis on which your examination answer is marked;

- suggest and provide some appropriate resources;

- assist you in planning and organising your work;

- check on your progress, reading written drafts and discussing ideas and issues which emerge from your own studies.

What is not legitimate is for someone other than you to produce an ideal response and for you and other students to learn and reproduce it under examination conditions. This malpractice clearly hampers the thinking of abler candidates, disadvantages weaker candidates when material is not understood properly, and penalises all candidates when that person has inadvertently introduced material deemed by examiners to be irrelevant.

How to structure an essay on life, death and life after death

A sound essay structure incorporates:

- a brief introduction

- accurate information

- a wide range of knowledge

- clear expression of ideas and understanding

- a variety of views

- examples in the main part of the essay

- evidence, analysis, perception and coherence in the conclusion.

Questions are normally structured in two parts. The first part tests your knowledge and understanding of a particular aspect of life, death and life after death. The second tests your analytical, critical and evaluative skills. Analytical skills are shown when you point out the complexity and compare different aspects of an issue or argument and consider to what extent they are supported by evidence and/or logic. Critical skills are demonstrated when you identify and explain arguments for and against a viewpoint or controversial statement and make a reasoned judgement about the accuracy or validity of those arguments. Evaluative skills are similar and are evident when you review the strengths and weaknesses of a viewpoint or balance two or more opinions on an issue and conclude with a reasoned personal opinion.

A basic structure for an answer is as follows:

Introduction	placing question/response in context, including definition/clarification of key terms; proposed method of tackling question, including stating areas to be used in answering question.
Main part	clearly separate responses to each part of the question; each area of study examined in turn; each paragraph having one major point, usually stated in the opening sentence of the paragraph; remainder of the paragraph consisting of elaboration, illustration, examination and/or application of that point.
Conclusion	in part (a), comparison and contrast of different relevant concepts within the areas used; in part (b), analysis of different viewpoints followed by a reasoned personal viewpoint based on the evidence presented.

What to avoid

A-level examiners have been impressed with the breadth and depth of knowledge, degree of understanding and perception in analysis shown by many candidates when tackling questions on life, death and life after death. However, the most prominent common weakness of the performance of candidates in recent years has been failure to demonstrate clearly connections between areas being examined. Amazingly, some candidates make no effort at all to make connections. Others concentrate on one area with literally only one or two brief references to a second area.

However extensive or excellent the material, an essay will be ungraded if it does not contain any explicit reference to two different areas of study. In such a case the candidate has failed to meet the requirement to draw together synoptically knowledge, understanding and skills. Where there is very little reference to a second area of study, the maximum award could be grade D, but is more likely to be grade E. It would depend on whether the quality of that reference was considered basic or only superficial.

Where the second area of study used in an answer is valid in its own right but is not within the content of the Religious Studies A-level Specification (e.g. sociology, anthropology, spiritualism), the maximum award is Level 3 – just over half marks. This is because candidates are demonstrating skills but not knowledge and understanding learned in different elements of their course of study, which is a requirement. However, where valid material from an area or areas outside the Specification content is included in addition to that from two areas of study within the Specification, no such restriction would apply. It should also be noted that identical perspectives/areas do not have to be referred to in responses to both parts of a question on life, death and life after death.

How to make connections

Explicit *comment* on connections between areas of study is essential for the award of Level 5 in part (a) of the essay. Such comment needs to be diverse, extensive or significant to warrant higher marks within the Level. One brief or banal comment would only justify the lowest mark within the Level. Making connections is achieved most impressively when candidates point out comparisons and contrasts throughout their answer. However, this is a complex task. Alternatively, in a structured essay, a substantial concluding paragraph in response to each part-question, highlighting main similarities and differences of relevant belief, concept, experience or practice between the areas, is often adequate.

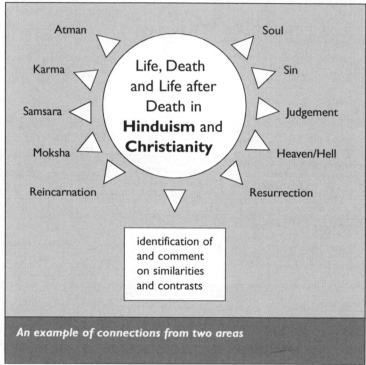

An example of connections from two areas

You should be aware that the use of examples from a different area does not constitute 'comment'. For example, if the concept of life after death (Philosophy of Religion) is merely illustrated by stories of resurrection (New Testament) that would not be deemed to constitute 'comment'. However, if a contrast was pointed out between forms of life after death found in different religions, say resurrection (Christianity) and reincarnation (Hinduism), then that would be valid comment on connections between areas of study.

Remember, the demand to comment on connections does not apply in part (b) where the emphasis is on the contribution of areas, not the connections between them.[1]

Writing task

Choose two areas of study. Brainstorm all the aspects of Life OR Death OR Life after Death that you can think of in these two areas and produce a spider diagram for each area. Then create a mind map showing the links between them.

---

[1] Many of the general principles in this chapter are found in 'Solving the Synoptic Problem' by Roger J. Owen in **Newyddion AG/RE News**, Issue 65, Spring 2003, p.4 and 'Achieving Synoptic Success' by Roger J. Owen in **Dialogue**, Issue 21, November 2003, pp. 27-30.

Chapter 2

The Nature and Purpose of Life

The ideas relating to human nature and our purpose within life are varied. The question of "What does it mean to be Human?" lies at the heart of most religious philosophies, whilst the answers can be seen through systems of belief and practice. In this chapter we shall examine some of the most important ideas related to this theme and consider their relevance for the different areas of study within the Religious Studies A-level course.

In this section we shall look at some of the main ideas about the origins of human beings. Many religions teach that human beings are the result of divine creation. This refers to the idea that all things within the universe derive the ultimate source of their being from God (or the Ultimate). The general traditions of the western religions hold that the universe was created 'ex nihilo' (out of nothing in Latin) and that the universe was specifically ordered for human life – seen as the pinnacle of creation by these traditions.

Christianity

Fundamental to the Christian understanding of human nature is the belief that the first humans were created in the image of God (imago Dei). This comes from Genesis 1:26-27, which states:

Then God said, 'Let us make man in our image, in our likeness,' . . . So God created man in his own image, in the image of God he created him; male and female he created them.

Man (and his nature) has been specifically designed by God, as a reflection or 'image' of God himself: thus all human beings possess, according to the teachings of Christianity, an inherent responsibility towards our Creator, to love and worship him. (This is a theme which is explicitly dealt with by St Thomas Aquinas in his moral theory of Natural Law.)

Judaism

Judaism sees God as the supreme creator, who created the universe and all life within it. This belief in creation provides Jews with an understanding of where, why and how they were created. The act of creation is described in the Torah. It shows the order and significance of creation and clearly points out the purpose and superiority of man.

God said to them ' . . . fill the earth and subdue it; and have dominion over . . . every living thing' . . . And it was so. God saw everything that he had made and, indeed, it was very good.

Islam

To Muslims, Allah is the sole Creator and Sustainer of the universe. He endows everything in creation with a purposeful nature. This 'nature' of creation sets limits, and

Research task

Research the seven characteristics that all living beings are supposed to possess, according to scientific understanding.
(You may find the following link helpful: http://www.bbc.tv/schools/gcsebitesize/biology - click on the 'Life processes' section)
- Choose which of these seven you think is the most important for Human Beings, and write down your answer.
- You should then share this in a class discussion. What ideas do people agree on? Where do you disagree?
- How do these characteristics relate to human beings as spiritual beings?
- Record the answers that are produced by the class.

this is one of the key points in the Qur'an. The Qur'an describes human nature as weak and needing guidance; man is viewed as rebellious and full of pride. Those who wish to be true Muslims recognise that they must submit themselves to the Divine will.

(God) is who created you, then fashioned you harmoniously and in due proportion; into whatsoever form he will he made you out of components ... He said: 'Our Lord is He Who gave to each (created) thing its form and nature, and further, gave (it) guidance.'

Discussion topic

How should being a product of Divine Creation affect the way a person behaves?

The following represents a brief summary of the Eastern religions' views on Creation and the place of mankind.

Buddhism

Within Buddhism, the idea of a Creator God (as it is traditionally held) is generally rejected, although many Buddhist traditions do make reference to Creation stories. The concept of a single, special event being the beginning of all existence is generally rejected. The phrase 'since beginningless time' is frequently used. The Big Bang may very well be the beginning of the current era in our local universe, but there is no reason to believe that it was anything other than just another link in the eternal chain of cause and effect. In summary, Buddhism rejects the whole idea of an identifiable origin of everything.

O disciples, there is a non-born, a non-produced, non-created and a non-formed. If there were not, O disciples, a non-born, a non-produced, a non-created and a non-formed, there would be no issue for the born, the produced, the created, the formed.

Hinduism

In Hindu philosophy, the existence of the universe is governed by the Trimurti of Brahma (the Creator), Vishnu (the Sustainer) and Shiva (the Destroyer). Hinduism has a specific understanding of how the world came to be, i.e. through the creative power of Brahma. After a time of preservation by Vishnu, this world will be destroyed by Shiva, before being 'created again'.

There is a concept within Hinduism of cyclic time, sometimes referred to as the days of Brahma. Time is believed to move in four billion year cycles, which is clearly different from the concept of linear time in many other religions. In Hinduism, nature and all of God's creations are manifestations of Him. He is within and without his creations. Thus all animals and humans have a divine element in them, but this is covered by ignorance and the illusions of our material existence.

The universe turns into minute (subtle) form at the time of dissolution and takes gross form at the time of creation. There was a universe before this one and there will be a universe after this one.

Sikhism

Sikhism affirms the belief in a Creator God and mankind's purpose is clearly tied towards serving this God. God is the perfect creator of the universe. The universe is not evil but contains evil; it is not suffering, but provides the soul with an opportunity to break free of the cycle of rebirth. This is what God wants for his creation and he gives them the opportunity to do this by recognizing his order in the universe. The role of the guru, who is the manifestation of God in the world, is to teach the means for prayer through the Guru Granth Sahib and the community of believers.

The Creator created himself ... And created all creation in which He is manifest. You Yourself are the bumble-bee, flower, fruit and the tree. You Yourself are the water, desert, ocean and the pond. You Yourself are the big fish, tortoise and the Cause of causes. Your form cannot be known.

What is Mankind's Purpose?

Summary

Bearing all of the above in mind, the question 'What does it mean to be human?' can be shown as having specific answers, depending on the religious tradition. However, whilst the content of each response may differ, what is certain is that religious traditions give a definite answer to the question. They believe firmly that there is a meaning to being human; that human beings have a role to play, within the created order – a role given (in most cases) by God (or The Ultimate).

Research task

Choose two of the areas of study that you intend to use for your Synoptic module. Research the specific teachings that relate to Creation within these modules and present your findings in the form of an extended piece of writing, where you comment upon the similarities and differences between them.

Product of chance?

For those who do not believe in the concept of a Creator God, an alternative view is that the universe is no more than the result of random chance. This is not a new idea, indeed it dates back many centuries, but it has come to the forefront in the past two hundred years. (Another alternative is the idea that the universe itself is eternal, has always existed and always will.) Such ideas have challenged traditional religious ideas about the world and mankind's place in it and this has led to observers reconsidering the possibility that the universe is no more than a random event.

Thinkers such as Dawkins and, opposing him, Stannard and Polkinghorne, have all commented on the relevance of the 'Big Bang' theory as a pointer that demonstrates that the universe is, indeed, a random event. There is no clear conclusion in this debate.

Stephen Hawking

The following points, made by Professor Stephen Hawking in *A Brief History of Time*, bear some consideration:

Einstein once asked the question: 'How much choice did God have in constructing the universe?'

Why does the universe go to all the bother of existing? ... does it need a creator, and, if so, does he have any other effect on the universe? And who created him?

... [we will be able to ask] the question of why it is that we and the universe exist. If we find the answer to that, it would be the ultimate triumph of human reason – for then we would know the mind of God.

Writing task

In what ways do you think Hawking's comments add to the debate of Divine Creation vs Random Chance? Write a response, either defending or opposing the belief in a universe created by Random Chance.

Definitions

Materialism: The belief that we are nothing more than a body (of which the mind is an integral, non-separate part), a physical entity that is complete within itself and having no need of a spirit or soul to make it complete – thus, for materialists, bodily death represents a definite end to our existence as individuals.

Dualism: The belief that we are composed of two distinct substances: one is our material body, the other is the mind/spirit/soul. Physical death only affects the material body and thus the mind/spirit/soul is able to survive this in some way.

Dualism

Beliefs about where we come from are, as we have seen, varied. However, the next question that can be asked is 'What are we?' If we are indeed 'created beings' then what exactly is our 'being'? Are we no more than a collection of chemicals which have produced a body of flesh, or is there something else? Just as materialism is usually associated with atheism, so dualism is more often associated with theism. It is therefore true to say that existence has a purpose beyond the ordinary hum-drum of life, and the ultimate fate of each person, as well as the world which we inhabit, does not have to be a meaningless existence ending in a total extinction.

From ancient cultures to biblical times, and throughout the course of human history, a belief has prevailed that humans are not just a 'body'. Even amongst eminent psychologists today there is a belief that human beings are at least both 'body' and 'mind' but religion would add 'soul' to that mix. What is the soul? Where does it come from?

Plato believed that the soul was an eternal, pre-existent form that became incarnated within the body at birth and then became a separate entity again, after physical death.

René Descartes considered the question of the relationship between body and soul and concluded that the mind was 'non-corporeal' (not of the body), a substance distinct from that of which the body itself was made.

In his *Principles of Philosophy* Descartes states:

... I knew that I was a substance the whole essence or nature of which was simply to think; and which, to exist, needs no place and has no dependence on any material thing ... that is to say my mind – what makes me what I am – [is] entirely distinct from my body.

Writing task

Consider the concept of dualism from the perspectives of two of your areas of study. How do these areas respond to such an idea? (e.g. in Ethics, does the possession of a separate body and soul affect the way a person might treat their body? In NT how does the theory of dualism relate to the Pauline concept of a bodily resurrection?)

Produce a set of notes which relate to dualism, from your areas of study.

Sanctity of life

All the major world religions agree that human life is special. Some elevate it to a unique status, with the Judeo-Christian traditions, enshrined within biblical literature, agreeing that humans are created *imago Dei* (in the image of God). What does it mean to be created in the image of God? Certainly it does not mean that humans look like God, for all monotheistic religions believe God to be incorporeal (non-physical). However, religious thinkers have found in this teaching a variety of other meanings, all of which give both special dignity and honour to the human race.

Related to the *imago Dei* is the belief that humans were created perfectly good (another concept on which the Western religions agree). The concept of original goodness is based partly on the creation of human beings in the image of God, but also on the theological point that God looked upon his creation of human beings and pronounced them 'very good'.

It is therefore no surprise that these traditions regard human life as particularly sacred. The eastern religious traditions would also agree with this, although they would further extend this definition to include all life, not just human. It is clear that there are major ramifications for the concept of religious ethics when these views of the sacredness of human life are taken on board. Issues such as abortion, euthanasia, war and pacifism, prejudice and discrimination, can all be interpreted through the lens of such belief.

With human life enjoying a position of prominence within the created order, it is therefore understandable that human beings have a certain level of responsibility to preserve, protect and promote an understanding of the special-ness/sacredness of human life, and also to ensure that quality of life is a key factor in their considerations. The concept of stewardship is related to this idea, as are similar concepts within all the various traditions. Religions *per se* enable human beings to see their place within the universe as one in which their role is of central importance.

The following scriptural quotations all relate to the concept of Sanctity of Life:

Christianity/Judaism

For it was you who formed my inward parts; you knit me together in my mother's womb ....in your book were written all the days that were formed for me, when none of them yet existed. Psalm 139:13, 16

Islam

We ordained for the children of Israel that if anyone slew a person ... it would be as if he slew the whole of mankind. And if anyone saved a life, it would be as if he saved the life of a whole people. Al-Ma'ida, 5:32

Hinduism

What is virtuous conduct? It is never destroying life, for killing leads to every other sin. pirukural 312, 321

Buddhism

As a mother with her own life guards the life of her own child, let all-embracing thoughts for all that lives be thine. Khuddaka Patha, Metta Sutta

Sikhism

This earth is a garden, The Lord its gardener, Cherishing all, none neglected. Adi Granth, Mahj Ashtpadi 1

Research task

For many people, the concept of 'Sanctity of Life' is closely tied up with that of 'Quality of Life'. Choosing two areas of study, find out what their viewpoints on the quality of life are. You should consider the following within your responses:

- Is it an intrinsic right of all human life?
- How is quality of life defined?
- What are the minimum requirements that might classify quality of life?
- How does it affect religious belief and practice?

Writing task

'During the next 35 years, the traditional view of the sanctity of human life will collapse under pressure from scientific, technological, and demographic developments. By 2040, it may be that only a rump of hard-core, know-nothing religious fundamentalists will defend the view that every human life, from conception to death, is sacrosanct.'
Peter Singer, *The Sanctity of Life*, 2005

Evaluate the contentions of the author in this quotation. You should make reference to at least two areas of study from RS9 in your answer.

Nature versus nurture

A debate which has relevance to the question of 'Who are we?' is the nature vs nurture debate. According to the teachings of the Roman Catholic Church, human beings possess a singular human nature, which is derived from being created *imago Dei*. This human nature is something which we can either fulfil (to the glory of God) or fall short of (sin). Our actions are given the merits of 'good' or 'bad' accordingly. This, however, is a typically Western theological view. The eastern view is somewhat different.

Within Buddhism, the idea that human beings consist of five skandhas suggests that there is no such thing as a single human nature, and that can pass through many forms, not just human. This would also be true of Hinduism, where the atman is representative of an individual's nature. The multiplicity of views as to what constitutes human nature, and what the consequences of possessing such nature are, has implications for our behaviour and development as individuals. If, for instance, we regard the idea that we have a 'God-given nature' then what does this imply for our ethical actions? Does this mean that there is an ideal form of behaviour which all human beings must live up to? If so, what is it?

As religion has struggled with the questions of the nature and purpose of human life, the sphere of science has taken a different route. Over the past two hundred years, scientific observations, from fields such as biology, psychology, sociology, psychiatry and anthropology, have all suggested that it is not just a simple matter of humans having a particular nature which they must attempt to fulfil (as claimed by philosophers such as Aristotle and Aquinas). These fields of study suggest instead that there are influences upon us, both individually and collectively, which have huge importance for our development – sometimes being the over-riding factors that determine who we are as fully fledged adults. These influences may come from families, friends, media and social groupings, but the common factor is that they are responsible for what we become. This is known as 'nurture' (indeed, one interpretation of 'nurture' might count all life experience as 'nurture').

Discussion topic

Compare and contrast ethical ideas about your aims/goals in life with those of religious adherents. You should make particular note of where they have ideas in common and where they differ.

It has been noted by several philosophers and theological commentators that the premise of the 'nature versus nurture' debate seems to negate the significance of free will. More specifically, if all our traits are determined by our genes, by our environment, by chance, or by some combination of these acting together, then there seems to be little room for free will. In any case, this line of reasoning suggests that the 'nature versus nurture' debate tends to exaggerate the degree to which individual human behaviour can be predicted, based on knowledge of genetics and the environment. In other words, if we are entirely determined by our biological programming, then there is no possibility that we can ever exercise 'free will' choices, as we can only ever act in the way that nature designed us!

Are we really free to make our own choices or are these already determined for us?

Free will vs determinism

What does it mean to have 'free will'? According to many philosophical commentators you need to be able to satisfy the following conditions:

1. We must have two or more possibilities genuinely open to us when we face a choice;
2. Our choice must not be forced in any way.

The concept of free will plays a central role in our thinking about the world, particularly in our apportioning of praise and blame, and in our finding people morally responsible for things they have done. Indeed, this idea is central to most religious thought systems which measure the deeds undertaken by an individual as either having merit or causing harm at some level. Concepts such as 'sin', 'karma' and 'duty' all presume the existence of human free will. By such free-will actions we either fulfil our duties or go against the precepts which have been given to us as spiritual beings.

The concept of determinism can create something of a paradox for us. If all things in the universe are 'determined' according to criteria which run the universe, then are our actions truly free? In other words, how do we know whether our actions are determined like the rising and setting of the sun, or whether the criteria by which we decide them are just less obvious to us!

Of course, the real paradox that exists within the debate is that free will can only exist within a framework of a determined universe, because otherwise how could we begin to predict the likely outcome of our actions? In other words, our free will must have potential to affect events around us and this can only happen in a regulated 'cause and effect' framework. It is this 'cause-effect' that underpins the concept of determinism.

The world religions have a variety of opinions on the concepts of both free will and determinism. It is also true to say that there are variations within each religion as to how far human beings actually possess free will and how far their lives have been determined.

Discussion topic

Consider the concept of free will from any two areas of study. How do they differ? Are there any similarities? Suggest reasons why this may be the case. How far does a belief in Predestination fit in, or conflict, with concepts such as ethical decision making, karma and individual freedom? Relate your answer to your areas of study.

As a point of comparison, some of the views from traditions within Buddhism and Islam are considered below:

Buddhism

Karma means our ability to create and to change.
It is creative because we can determine how and why we act.
We can change.

The Tibetan Book of Living and Dying

Whilst a prevailing sense of karma permeates the belief system of the Buddhist, the notion of free will is seen as enabling the Buddhist to choose to overcome the karmic cycle and release the self to enlightenment. The controversial writer, F. Lenz, remarked:

That is what free will really is.
It is the ability to alter the sequence of karmic fate
that was about to become our future.

Surfing the Himalayas (F. Lenz, 1997)

However, it should also be borne in mind that there are those within the Buddhist tradition who believe that free will, as understood by our previous definitions, is actually an illusion and that our actions of today are the result of 'karmic effect' from the past. This is only true for those who exist at the unenlightened level – once enlightenment has been gained, the law of karma ceases to be applicable and the actions of the enlightened one are truly actions of free will.

Islam

Beliefs within Islam relating to both free will and determinism are often misinterpreted by those outside the tradition. Many think that all Muslims believe in predestination over free will, but that is to misunderstand a fundamental distinction that relates to the nature of both Allah and mankind. A Muslim must believe in the divine will - *qadar* in Arabic. The concept of *qadar* means that when Allah created each thing, he determined when it would come into existence and when it would cease to exist. He also determined its nature and qualities. And everything in the universe, the seen and the unseen, is completely subject to the overriding power of Allah. Nothing can happen outside his will.

Points for consideration

- *Our actions will always have consequences, but how should this affect the way in which our lives are lived?*
- *Are our actions recorded on a universal scale i.e. by a divine being?*

As for human beings, they are not in complete control of their own destinies, but neither are they mindless automatons whose every action is controlled by some 'unseen hand'. Allah gave humans limited power and great freedom, including the freedom of choice. That ability to have choice makes each individual accountable for his or her actions. From the view of Islam, human beings are free. A person has no excuse for making the wrong choice and then blaming *qadar* or destiny, any more than a man hitting a wall with his head can blame the laws of nature. He obviously understood what the consequences of his actions would be and must not therefore expect something different to happen other than to experience the pain of doing so!

A biblical view

It is also true to say that the Bible contains several passages which promote both free will and determinism. The creation stories and the passages relating to the Fall expound a concept of free will; but the Psalms (e.g. Psalm 139) contain hints of determinism – as do the many accounts of the prophets, when they warn of what will follow if the chosen people do not return to the ways of righteousness.

In the NT, although free will is an assumed concept, many of the prophecies contained within the Synoptic Gospels suggest determinism. Being free, in the NT, is largely related to the idea of freedom from sin – a recurring message in the letters of St Paul. The fact that a person is able to turn away from sin and be reborn again in the Holy Spirit (cf John 3, and Jesus' conversation with Nicodemus) seems to suggest that free will is assured and overrides any concept of determinism. However, Calvin and others have interpreted much of the NT to suggest that God has pre-determined the destiny of all humans (e.g. Romans 8:29). This creates a tension within the NT between the two concepts – one which cannot easily be resolved.

Why do we exist?

This greatest of ultimate questions has no single, or easy, answer. All religions give answers to it, and some of those answers have been considered, by implication, in the material above. However, all religions agree that what we do in this life has some kind of impact or effect on the next life. Whether that next life be a rebirth, reincarnation or sustained existence within a place of eternal happiness or suffering, what we do in the here and now has some bearing on it. That is why many regard this life as preparation for the next – not as a side issue but as an essential one. This does not mean that a kind of fatalistic approach to our existence should be adopted – indeed all religions agree that this life is in many ways a precious gift and one that should not be squandered on speculative hopes for the future, to be gained at the expense of the present. However, this life, lived to its fullest – in all of the senses considered above – should serve as a preparation for the journey into the next, whatever that may be.

Writing task

Using material from at least two areas of study, write an outline answer to the question: 'What is the nature and purpose of human life?'

Suggested essay outline

Introduction

▼

What does it mean to be human? Examples from areas of study

▼

How different areas of study compare and contrast in their ideas of what it means to be human – at least two areas should be compared/contrasted (eg Creation vs Chance, Nature vs Nurture, Free will vs Determinism, etc.)

▼

General conclusion – highlighting the main ideas already presented in the essay and restating some of the main points of comparison/contrast

Chapter 3

Different Ideas about the Significance of Death

Introduction

Whoever we are and whatever background we come from, whatever life we lead and whatever belief system we follow, we all have one thing in common – we die. Whether that death is the end, or a doorway, or a transition, we do not know for certain, but our faith systems provide answers. It is to these answers that we now turn our attention.

In this chapter we shall consider some of the main ideas about the significance of death and how these ideas are shown through the various customs and rituals that mark the passing of life. It should be borne in mind that, due to cultural differences, many of these customs may vary, according to where one lives.

The ideas that the various traditions have about death and what may lie beyond, as well as the understanding of what the purpose of this life is, can be seen through the rituals associated with death, often referred to as 'funerals' or 'death rites'. We shall consider the main issues from the standpoint of the six major world religions.

Buddhism

As life is seen as a state of impermanence, it is of no surprise that death within Buddhism is viewed in much the same way. The monastic community play an important part in the rituals associated with dying and death in Buddhism. When a person is dying, members of the Sangha (if available, otherwise it will be a lay Buddhist) gather round the dying person and chant hymns, prayers and scriptures, as a reminder to the dying person that death is but one step within the wheel of rebirth. This is done in order to calm the person and help them prepare for their death in a suitable manner. It is believed that the way in which a person dies will influence their next rebirth, so it is important that their mind is as calm as possible.

Once the person has died, the body is ritually washed and prepared. It is then placed into a coffin. In Buddhism the normal method of disposing of the body is cremation. The coffin is covered with brightly coloured flowers and, where possible, taken to the nearest temple. Here it is placed in front of a statue of the Buddha and blessings are said. The actual funeral ceremony is meant to be a happy one. Monks recite scriptures, to remind all present of the impermanence of existence and to comfort the mourners. Sometimes prayers are written on pieces of paper and hung near the coffin. It is important that, following the death of the loved one, those who were close to them remember them in prayers. Sometimes memorial services are held after the funeral service. This happens particularly when it is the funeral of a parent: the child will hold a memorial service 100 days after the death, to allow them time to get over their grief and to properly remember the parent in a positive way. Thanks are given for their life at this service. All of these remembrances are important as they help the dead person achieve a good rebirth.

Christianity

Within Christianity, death is not seen as the end of life, but rather as the doorway into the next life. As God created all to have a personal relationship with him, it is through making the transition from this life to the next that that relationship can become fully realised.

In primitive forms of Christianity, the service held for a person who had died was always joyful. The hope of resurrection and being taken into God's kingdom as a reward for faith was a real inspiration for a community that often found this earthly existence harsh by comparison – particularly when they were enduring persecution. By the time that Christianity had become an established part of the Roman Empire, such joy was not always deemed appropriate and services became far more sombre. By the Middle Ages this had developed into a full blown ceremony, with prayers for the dead said throughout the night prior to burial, and a full requiem mass being common practice on the day that the person was buried.

Preparation of the body for burial is usually done by specialist undertakers in Western Christianity. There are variations of this and it is more common for family members to be involved in the preparation of the body in Eastern Christianity. Cultural norms tend to be adopted at this time: the body is usually put into smart, clean clothes or it may be wrapped in a clean white cloth. After this it will be placed into a coffin and laid somewhere suitable such as a chapel of rest. Traditionally this is the time when mourners will pay their last respects to the deceased, saying prayers for the dead person and commending their soul to God. This is especially important in the Roman Catholic tradition, where the belief in purgatory is held.

Research task

Praying for the dead is a common feature of most religious traditions. Identify the key features of such prayers and, relating them to their religious tradition, show how they illustrate belief in that religion about the significance of death.

Whilst burial was, and in some forms of Christianity still is, the accepted norm, cremation has become an acceptable alternative. For most Christians it is a matter of personal choice as to which they choose.

Research task

In preparation for death, the Roman Catholic priest will often administer the Last Rites (Viaticum). Find out exactly what is involved in this ritual and why it is so important for the Roman Catholic believer.

Over the past few years, the structure of the funeral service within western Christianity has become more flexible. This is especially true in those churches which do not have formalised liturgies. This flexibility allows for the deceased's personal wishes to be included within their funeral service, which personalises it and allows the family and friends to feel as if the service truly reflects and celebrates the life of the deceased. The actual ceremony will differ according to denomination, although common features of the funeral ceremony in Christianity are: prayers for the dead; scripture readings, usually including Psalms (Psalm 23 is used particularly in this context); a short speech, by either the priest/minister or a close member of the family, where the dead person is remembered; and the singing of hymns. The Roman Catholic tradition will often celebrate a requiem mass during this service.

After the ceremony, the coffin will be taken, either to the crematorium or to the graveside. At both places a short service of committal will take place. During this, prayers will again be said and scripture will again be recited. If it is a burial, it is traditional for mourners to throw earth onto the coffin after it has been lowered into the ground. In some traditions, a few flowers will also be thrown. Following the burial or cremation, the family and friends will usually gather together at the dead person's home in order to share their remembrances of the deceased.

There is no fixed mourning period within Christianity. However, it is traditional to remember the dead on the anniversary of their deaths and especially on All Saints Day, when some traditions will hold a requiem mass to remember all those who have died in the recent past.

Research task

Using a suitable biblical concordance, record what the New Testament has to say about death and its significance. This should then be used as a basis for explaining the Christian rituals associated with death.

A Christian funeral in a graveyard

Hinduism

Belief in a cyclical reincarnation of the soul is key to Hinduism. Death is regarded as a natural part of life. Within Hindu scripture there are many descriptions of the reason for death's existence, and the rituals that should be performed surrounding it, as well as the possible destinations of the soul once it has passed from this current earthly incarnation. Whilst Moksha (see Chapter 4) is the ultimate goal, Hindus believe that the next life that they will experience will be directly connected to their experience of this life – and the way in which they have lived it.

In Hinduism, cremation is not just seen as a way in which to consume the body, but is essential for releasing the soul from that body. The funeral pyre also symbolizes an offering to Agni, the god of fire, through which the blessing of the gods is gained, enabling the soul to be looked upon more favourably as it prepares for its next incarnation.

Worshipping the fire god, Agni, at a temple in India

All of the rituals associated with death in Hinduism demonstrate that death is not to be feared. In common with other Eastern religions, e.g. Sikhism, excessive grief is not encouraged, as it is seen as a distraction to the soul of the one who has just died, preventing it from finding the way to its next birth. Hindus are thus taught to love death in the same way that they love life – it is all part of the karmic wheel of samsara.

Islam

Death is not feared in Islam, but is seen as the gateway into life eternal. Indeed, within Islam the belief in life after death not only guarantees success in the afterlife, but also encourages Muslims in this life to make the most of the opportunities that it brings – in order to show their submission to the will of Allah and, through their duty, prove themselves worthy of a place in paradise. As at all significant times in the life of the Muslim, reciting the Shahadah is seen as an important part of the preparation for death. Either the dying person will say it themselves, or a close relative will say it for them, if they are unable to. In this way the person is fully prepared for death.

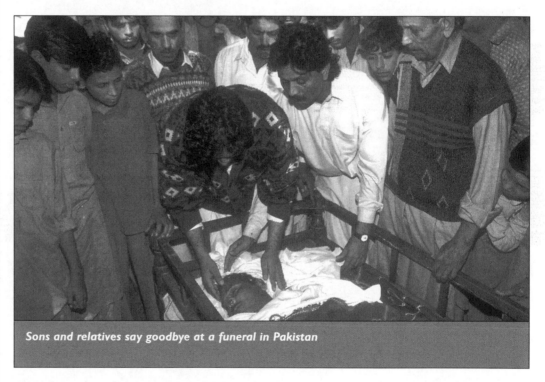

Sons and relatives say goodbye at a funeral in Pakistan

Once the person has died, their body is ritually washed (known as Ghusl) and prepared for burial. This is usually done by members of the family, of the same sex as the deceased. Muslims see this as a last service that they can perform for their loved one, but it also provides them with a reminder of their own mortality. The body is wrapped in a clean white cloth, in a manner somewhat similar to the clothes worn by pilgrims on Hajj. The symbolism is the same: all are equal in death and before Allah. Once prepared, the body is taken to a suitable clean place (referred to as salah-ul-janazah), usually outside, where special prayers for the dead are recited. These are led by the Imam, who stands near the head of the dead person, facing away from the mourners.

One important feature of Islamic funeral rites is that burial must always occur as soon as possible after the person has died – usually within 24 hours. It is also important that the dead person is buried in an area set aside for Muslims and facing towards the Kab'ah in

Makkah. Muslims believe that the body must be laid in direct contact with the earth, so traditionally coffins are not used in Islam. However, in countries such as the UK, where laws do not allow for burials without a coffin, Muslims are allowed to invert the coffin so that, whilst the body has contact with the earth, it is mostly covered by the coffin. It is seen as inappropriate for Muslims to spend vast amounts of money on a funeral, as they believe that the money can be better applied to those who are living and in need.

The mourning period in Islam tends to be 3 days, during which somber clothing is worn. The mourners spend time in prayer and receive condolences. According to the teachings of the Qur'an, women who lose their husbands tend to have an extended mourning period, referred to as iddah, which lasts for 4 months and 10 days.

Discussion topic

Many of the Islamic rituals involved in death are echoed throughout the five pillars, particularly Shahadah, Salah and Hajj. What do you think this tells us about the way in which Muslims see death?

Judaism

In Judaism the Shema should be the final words that are said by a person as they die. Once they have passed away it is customary for the mourners to make a small tear in their clothing. In biblical times, rending the garments as a sign of grief was common practice: it is in memory of this that the tear is made, but it also shows that the person has been 'torn away' from those still living.

For Jews, burial should follow soon after death. The practice of cremation is forbidden, because it is seen as destroying that which God has made, and also because the deceased cannot then be resurrected on Judgement Day. In preparation for burial the body is washed by members of the same sex, and then carefully wrapped in a simple cloth and placed into a plain coffin. This symbolises that all are equal in death, no matter what their standing in life. It is also seen as disrespectful to leave the body between the times of death and burial, and so it will be attended at all times during this period, usually by close family, although it can be by friends as well.

The actual funeral service is very short. During this the Rabbi will usually give a short speech, psalms will be read and prayers said. As the coffin is lowered into the earth, the mourners present will scatter earth on top of the coffin. Following this they will wash their hands and then leave the cemetery. It is customary for Jews to be buried in areas separate from non-Jews.

Research task

Using a suitable biblical concordance, record what the bible has to say about death and its significance for understanding the Jewish rituals associated with death.

Although customs vary, a common form of marking the passing of the loved one is to serve hard-boiled eggs when the mourners return home from the cemetery. This is meant to symbolise the fact that, like the egg which is not opened, the grief of the mourners can not be expressed through words.

The first week after death is known as shiva. This is an intense period of mourning where the mourners will sit on low chairs to show their grief. During this time they will recite special prayers several times a day. Mourners are encouraged to talk about their feelings of grief during this time, to help them deal with it. It is also a time of abstinence: mirrors in the house are all covered

Discussion topic

What do you think are the benefits of a set mourning period, such as shiva?

and music will not be listened to. Normal vanities (brushing hair, cutting nails, etc.) are forsaken, and sexual activity is forbidden during this time. It is also customary not to wear shoes made of leather. A solitary candle is kept alight during the whole period of shiva, both day and night. Once the week is over, the mourners are encouraged to put away their grief and resume their normal lives, although a simple memorial is usually held by the mourners, one year on.

Sikhism

The 5 Ks play an integral part in the preparation of the body for the funeral rite. The body is washed and dressed in clean clothes and then adorned with the 5 Ks. During this preparation of the body it is also common practice for hymns from the Guru Granth Sahib to be read aloud. After preparation, the body may either be kept at home or taken to the gurdwara – this is usually a matter of choice but allows everyone in the community to pay their respects to the dead person.

Sikh women pray over the open coffin before the funeral

Once respects have been paid, the coffin is covered and a procession towards the place of cremation takes place. In countries where it is possible, this will be a walking procession to the funeral pyre. Where this is not possible (such as in the UK), friends and relatives drive in procession to the crematorium. Upon arrival at the place of cremation, the Kirtan Sohila is recited, followed by the Ardas, which sends blessings to the soul that has departed. The funeral pyre is then lit by a close relative – usually the son (if appropriate).

In the UK the body is burnt in a crematorium rather than a pyre. An interesting feature of Sikh funerals is that no memorial is allowed to be left at the place where the body is burnt. Sikhs believe that, as the soul never truly dies, there should be no grief at the funeral service, so it is forbidden to mark the place of cremation. When the ashes of the deceased have been collected they are usually scattered into flowing water. For those Sikhs who live near the sea, it is here that the ashes will be scattered.

Following the cremation, friends and relatives will gather at the home of the deceased's family, where they will begin the Akhand Path (a complete reading of the Guru Granth Sahib). This can take 48 hours to complete, but tends to be done over the ten day mourning period set aside by Sikhism. The family and friends are allowed to show grief here, but it should not be excessive, for the reasons already stated above.

Sikhs are taught not to be afraid of death. They believe that the duty of all Sikhs is to move from self-centeredness (that behaviour which locks a person into the cycle of birth, death and rebirth) towards God-centeredness (where the soul achieves Moksha and becomes united with God). This is why the funeral and mourning period should reflect a positive note, for none truly die. The person lives on in the words and deeds – a fact that is recorded within the Guru Granth Sahib. Death, then, is seen not as the end but as the gateway into another life.

Discussion topic

- Why do you think it is important for Sikhs to avoid an excessive amount of grief during the mourning period?
- How do you think this affects their outlook on life in general?

Whose life is it anyway?

The question that is usually asked is: 'Whose life is it anyway?' and the response that is given is essential in determining the individual's attitude towards issues such as euthanasia and suicide.

Writing task

Write a short paragraph on each of these terms:
- Quality of Life
- Sanctity of Life

Research task

Use the internet to find out the main views for and against euthanasia. You should collect your information in a table form (for/against).

Euthanasia is currently illegal in the UK, although suicide is not, but there have been a number of attempts to change the legal position. In 2003 the House of Lords gave two readings to the Patient (Assisted Dying) Bill, the summary of which states:

This bill would enable a competent adult who is suffering unbearably as a result of a terminal or a serious and progressive physical illness to receive medical help to die at his own considered and persistent request; and make provision for a person suffering from such a condition to receive pain relief medication.

At the time of writing, this bill, which has attracted much controversy from a range of secular as well as religious groups, has not been passed.

Discussion topic

Read the summary of the bill again. Using this and the other information that you have collected, organise a class debate on whether euthanasia should be legalised.

The sanctity of life is a very important principle within the sphere of religion and most of the major world religions directly oppose euthanasia. As God has given life to the believer, the theistic religions would state that euthanasia takes away that which only

21

God can take. Buddhism adopts a principle of 'no harm' (ahimsa) and therefore will usually state that euthanasia is wrong although, in certain circumstances, it is permissible.

There also exist groups within each of the religious traditions that believe it is not just simply a matter of prohibiting euthanasia, and that there are occasions when it can be seen as the lesser of two evils. The debate is extremely complex.

Research/writing tasks

- Drawing on material from the areas you have studied, prepare a power-point presentation which evaluates how death is viewed within the selected areas. You should make use, where appropriate, of images and sound to enhance your presentation.

- Choose any two areas and draw up a list of similarities and difference between them. You should include details of the way they view death and other rituals that are carried out to mark this important rite of passage.

- Write an information guide for people working in a hospital. This should outline how a person may be treated once they have died. You should include a list of 'do's' and 'don'ts and include a section that might help those in the hospital to relate effectively to grieving relatives.

Chapter 4

Different Ideas about Life after Death

Introduction

As we have seen from the previous chapters, views on Life and Death are varied and complex. This chapter endeavours to look at some of the main concepts relating to what religious systems have to say about Life after Death.

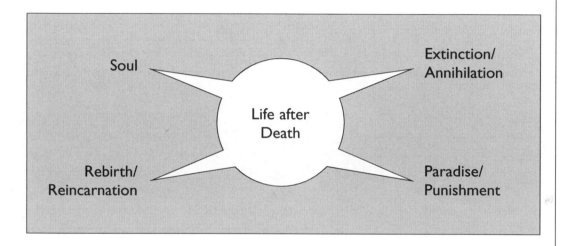

Within the historical western religious traditions (and the philosophical and ethical ideas associated with them) there has long been the concept of an 'after-life'. This after-life is seen as an extension to the current existence, where the individual retains some part of his/her earthly identity. This identity (i.e. that which makes a person in some way recognisable and unique) is often, although not exclusively, seen as the 'soul' and it is through this vehicle of the 'soul' that the individual passes into the after-life. Another concept is that of judgement, whereby the individual is judged on the actions of their earthly existence and, if the right conditions have been met, according to the specifications of the religion concerned, will pass into paradise. If the reverse is true, then a place of punishment awaits the unworthy.

The eastern religious traditions have a different approach to this area of belief. One common feature, it could be argued, is the existence of a 'soul' which houses the person's 'identity' but that is as far as it goes (and some Buddhists would even disagree with that). The basic idea is that after death (again according to what the actions of the individual in life have been) the soul then moves on to another body and is reborn. Hindus and Buddhists disagree as to how much of the person's original identity is passed on to this 'next life', but there is a definite move from one incarnation to another. The exception is if the individual finds release from this cycle and achieves a state best described as 'extinction from self awareness'.

In the following pages we shall look at some of these concepts in more detail; it should also be borne in mind that many of the religious traditions contain great variations in the acceptance of these beliefs. As it not possible to address everything in a short book, the beliefs discussed below tend to be those that are most widely accepted.

Reincarnation

The belief that somehow we are born, die and are reborn into new bodies, is one of the most prevalent religious ideas that exists. It is taught throughout the eastern religions, in one form or another but, to some people's surprise, can also be found within the Western traditions – although not necessarily officially recognised.

Within the **Buddhist** tradition, the idea of 'Rebirth' is that the non-material mind survives bodily death. The mind is effectively drawn towards its next rebirth as a direct consequence of the karmic actions of previous incarnations, a process known as 'uncontrolled rebirth'. An aim of Buddhist meditation is to focus the mind and purify it from previous negative karmic imprints, thus maintaining some control over the process of rebirth and trying to avoid the worst sorts of rebirth.

According to the main teachings of Buddhism, there is no permanent and unchanging soul and there is no movement of soul from one body to the next, in the strictest sense. However, as Buddhism never rejected samsara (see later in this chapter for an extended explanation of this concept) there is debate over what is transmitted between lives.

In spite of the teachings in Buddhism against the idea of a soul, Tibetan Buddhists do believe that a new-born child may be the reincarnation of someone departed. In Tibetan Buddhism the soul of an important lama (like the Dalai Lama) is supposed to pass into an infant born nine months after his death.

Within **Hinduism**, the idea of reincarnation (or the transmigration of the soul) was established from ancient times. It can be found within the Upanishads, which reflect earlier ideas found in the original Vedas. The belief that the soul reincarnates is intricately linked to karma, which says that individual souls, or atmans, pass from one plane of existence and carry with them impressions from their former existences. These are taken to the next life and result in an existence which is directly caused by the karmic actions of the previous existences.

Reincarnation is not recognized by **Islam** – and has even been declared blasphemy by at least one authority – but some commentators believe that it is accepted within the Sufi tradition. According to those who suggest that reincarnation is implicitly referred to within scripture, its basis in the Qu'ran includes Sura 2:28:

How can you deny God,
when you were dead and God gave you life?
Then God will cause you to die, and then revive you,
and then you will be returned to God .

Other Muslims would counter this idea with reference to verses like those found in Sura 37:58-61

Is it (the case) that we shall not die, except our first death,
And that we shall not be punished?
Verily this is the supreme achievement!
For the like of this let all strive, who wish to strive.

The belief in Reincarnation is also present within the **Jewish** tradition, where it is referred to as *gilgul*. This became popular in folk belief, and is found in much Yiddish literature among Ashkenazi Jews. While many Jews today do not believe in reincarnation, the belief is common amongst Orthodox Jews, particularly amongst Hasidim; some Hasidic siddurim (prayerbooks) have a prayer asking for forgiveness for the sins that one may have committed in this *gilgul* or a previous one.

Interestingly, Reincarnation is also found in some traditions of early **Christianity** and, whilst most references to it have been purged from 'official' Church documentation, evidence can be found within the teachings of early Celtic Christianity. The Synod of Whitby in 664 denounced this form of Christianity, but much of its teaching lived on, notably within the philosophies of Irish philosopher Johannes Scotus Erigena. The Early Church Fathers, Origen and Clement of Alexandria, are also seen as supporting this view. Gregory of Nyssa quotes Origen:

By some inclination toward evil, certain souls ... come into bodies, first of men; then through their association with the irrational passions, after the allotted span of human life, they are changed into beasts, from which they sink to the level of plants. From this condition they rise again through the same stages and are restored to their heavenly place.

B.W. Butterworth, *On First Principles*, Book I, Chapter VIII New York: Harper & Row, 1966, p. 73

Discussion topics

- Why do you think the idea of reincarnation is so widespread?
- Are there any obvious psychological advantages for people of religion in accepting this teaching?
- Why do you think orthodox forms of Christianity and Islam reject the idea?

Samsara

There are various interpretations of precisely what is meant by Samsara in the different traditions of Buddhism, Hinduism and Sikhism. Whilst the prevailing view is that it is a cycle to be escaped, there also exist interpretations which see it as illusory or merely symbolic. Hinduism sometimes translates the idea of Samsara as ignorance of the True Self, where the soul falls into believing that the current, temporal, world is the real one and thus becomes trapped into the cycle of samsara. This is known as *Avidya*, or ignorance of one's true self, and it is this that leads one to be caught up in the chains of desire, karma and reincarnation. This state of being is known as *Maya*. It is only through Moksha (see below) that one can escape this cycle.

Within Sikhism the idea, which is virtually identical to the one expressed in Hinduism, has been explained by using the analogy of shedding clothes which no longer fit (death) and putting on new clothing (rebirth). In other words, the soul leaves its old body and finds a new one. Death is nothing to be feared in Sikhism as the soul never truly dies – it is either reborn or it finds unity with God.

Buddhism was founded on a rejection of concepts such as that of the 'self' or 'atman' and instead sees the self as being composed of the 5 skandhas, which reform after each rebirth.

The Tibetan Wheel of Life

The self...was dependent on the coming together of five skandhas or bundles, all of which are changing. These skandhas are Form (the body), Sensations, Perceptions, Mental formations (impulses and habits) and Consciousness. None of these could be described as the soul or essence of the person, not even consciousness....Because the self is dependent on these five changing skandhas, it is itself in flux, dependent and impermanent. (p29)

Later schools of Buddhism re-introduce the concept of a 'person' which transmigrates. However, the basic idea that there is a cycle of birth and rebirth is not questioned in early Buddhism and its successors; neither, generally, is the concept that Samsara is a negative condition, to be escaped through religious practice which results in the achievement of Nirvana.

Moksha, the Sanskrit word for liberation, or *Mukti*, the Sanskrit word for release, refer, generally speaking, to gaining freedom from the cycle of death and rebirth. Within Hinduism the atman (or self) is 'released' from the cycle of Samsara, freed from the shackles of this world; in this loss of identity of self, the atman becomes united with Brahman, the 'universal soul' (although this concept is not be confused with the Western idea of a personal God).

It is important to realise that this is an entirely different goal from that which is aspired to by religions such as Christianity and Islam. There is no soteriological (salvation) aspect to Moksha: it is the loss of the ego, or self, which is the highest goal for a system which sees the constant reincarnation of the self as something to be escaped. Within Sikhism, however, Moksha is seen as the soul breaking free from the cycle of birth and death to return to God. It is generally agreed that the concepts of Moksha/Mukti are not identical to Nirvana within Buddhism, although in Jainism (an offshoot of Hinduism) the concepts are identical.

Writing task

Explain why you think a person who believes in reincarnation/rebirth would see an eventual release from this cycle as something to be aimed for.
How do you think this differs from the idea of those who believe nothing happens to a person after they die, that death is the end?

Resurrection

The teachings of Christianity, based on the words of the New Testament, are that Resurrection is the destiny of all those who die '. . . in the faith of Christ . . .'. Not only does the NT say this, but primitive statements of Christian belief, such as the 4th Century Apostle's Creed, also maintain it: '*I believe in the resurrection of the Body, the life everlasting . . .*'

Pilgrims at the Garden Tomb, Jerusalem

Resurrection is the rising again from the dead, the resumption of life. The New Testament makes many references to the concept of resurrection, from the teachings of Jesus (e.g. Luke 14:14; John 5:28-29; 6:39-40; 11:25) to the Letters of St Paul (1 Corinthians 15:12; Philippians 3:21; 1 Thessalonians 4:14-16; 2 Timothy 2:11; Hebrews 6:2) through to the Apocalyptic visions of St John (Revelation 20:12).

Jesus is recorded as having been raised from the dead on the third day after his Crucifixion. This is seen by many Christians today as the central tenet of their faith and forms the basis of the Atonement theory (i.e. the idea that Jesus died to save people from their sins). It is therefore a central concept in the teachings of Christianity.

However, some also say that the idea of a Resurrection is present within certain parts of the Old Testament as well; for instance, scholars argue that the account of Ezekiel and the dry bones which are brought back to life (Ezekiel 37: 1-14) would not have been intelligible to an audience who were not already familiar with a resurrection concept. The Book of Job also raises the idea at the midpoint of his sufferings, in 19: 25-27:

For I know that my Redeemer lives, And He shall stand at last on the earth: And after my skin is destroyed, this I know, That in my flesh I shall see God, Whom I shall see for myself, And my eyes shall behold, and not another. How my heart yearns within me ...

Resurrection is therefore affirmed within the biblical accounts. This belief is also affirmed in a wide variety of early Christian literature, represented by the following examples:

For the Church, although dispersed throughout the whole world even to the ends of the earth, has received from the apostles and from their disciples the faith in ... the raising up again of all flesh of all humanity, in order that to Jesus Christ our Lord and God and Savior and King, in accord with the approval of the invisible Father, every knee shall bend of those in heaven and on earth and under the earth, and that every tongue shall confess him, and that he may make just judgment of them all.

Irenaeus, *Against Heresies* 1:10:1–4 [A.D. 189]

Perish the thought that the omnipotence of the Creator is unable, for the raising of our bodies and for the restoring of them to life, to recall all [their] parts, which were consumed by beasts or by fire, or which disintegrated into dust or ashes, or were melted away into a fluid, or were evaporated away in vapors.

Augustine, *The City of God* 22:20:1 [A.D. 419]

Research task

Using a biblical concordance, compile a list of passages which mention the concept of Resurrection. Use these passages in your synoptic essay to support your writing.

Judgement

This is a key theme for Christianity, Islam and Judaism. In **Christianity** it is believed that the judgement of mankind will be announced by the trumpet call of the angels (Matthew 24:31). The earlier teaching in the Sermon on the Mount also indicates that those who fall into sin will not be saved, but will be cast into hell. This is reinforced in Revelation 20:14. However for the righteous, the Heavenly Jerusalem is described:

I saw the Holy City, the new Jerusalem, coming down out of heaven from God, prepared as a bride beautifully dressed for her husband. And I heard a loud voice from the throne saying, 'Now the dwelling of God is with men, and He will live with them. They will be his people, and God Himself will be with them and be their God.'

This judgement will occur at the end of time (an event known as the Eschaton) and it will involve God's final and lasting judgement on Mankind, both corporately and individually.

Islam also has a trumpet blast to herald the last judgement. The righteous will go to Paradise or Janah, where gardens of delight await them (see below for more detail). The wicked infidels will be cast into Hell, where they live an eternity in torment (Sura 14:50 and Sura 74:21).

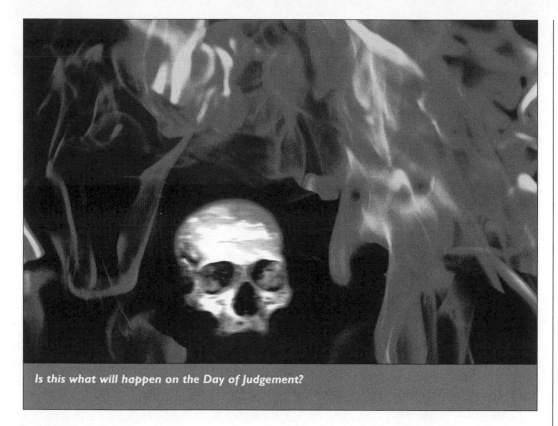
Is this what will happen on the Day of Judgement?

Judaism shares the trumpet blast, in the form of the Shofar being sounded to announce the beginning of the Messianic era. All will be gathered together to the heavenly court for the Day of Judgement. The righteous will reside in Gan'eden (heaven) whilst the unrighteous will be sent to Gehinnon, where they will burn for all eternity.

Thus the three Western religions share common themes when it comes to Judgement day. The details may vary, but all three agree that there is a causal link between behaviour in this world and destination in the next. It should be acknowledged, however, that whilst the views above represent the traditional views of those religions, there does exist a variety of opinion on the place of hell. Within both Christianity and Judaism, there exists the belief that eternal punishment is not the action of a loving God. Thus some believe that the punishment is temporary i.e. until the sins of this life have been paid for. Others believe that Hell as a place does not exist at all, as it is incompatible with belief in a good God.

Eternal life

The places of reward or punishment in the Western traditions are seen as everlasting. Unlike this existence, which is temporary, our next is to be eternal. This means that the believer will exist forever, in the realm that they have determined for themselves by the choices they have made in this lifetime, according to the dictates of their faith system.

Within Christianity, the concept of eternal life is recognised by some as starting when the believer accepts Christ and participates in the Kingdom of God, through obedience to Christ's commands. C. H. Dodd called this idea 'realised eschatology' (as opposed to 'final eschatology', outlined at the beginning of this section, which is generally seen as the accepted model within the Old Testament part of the Christian Bible, as well as in the Pauline epistles). The place of heaven is one of fellowship with others and god (Revelation 21:3), eternal worship and praise of god (Rev 19v1-6), in joyful service to the throne of the most high.

Is this the journey to Heaven?

In Judaism, heaven, or *Gan'eden*, is where faithful Jews will live eternally, enjoying the radiance of the divine presence – a concept very similar to that of Christianity. The Islamic view of eternal life is one of sensual pleasure, as shown in this quotation from Sura 55:56:

On couches with linings of brocade shall [the faithful Muslim] recline, and therein shall be the damsels with retiring glances, whom nor man nor djinn hath touched before them: Like jacinth and pearls: Shall the reward of good be aught but good? And beside these shall be two other gardens: With gushing fountains in each: In each fruits and the palm and the pomegranate.

Sheol

In the Old Testament, the word 'Sheol' is used to describe the place where the dead can be found: but what exactly is it? This is a matter of some debate. Is it a place where the dead go to in order to 'live on'? Or is it nothing more than a term for the grave, wherein all dead bodies are laid? The concept of Sheol has been occasionally confused with that of Hell, but this is a misunderstanding. The New Testament appears to contrast the idea of Sheol with that of *Gehinnom*, or *Gehenna*, which seems to be closer to the concept of Hell, i.e. a place of condemnation.

The meaning of the word 'Sheol' seems to vary from 'a place for the dead' to 'an underworld' and the idea of 'the grave'. Despite these characteristics as a 'shadowy existence', it is a place where God still rules, as if it were an extension of the earthly realm of the living.

In the New Testament, the parable of the Rich Man and Lazarus also makes reference to Sheol, but here it is seen as a place of torment, which is perhaps why in some translations it is given the title *Hades* (a reflection of the Greek idea which parallels Sheol as a realm of the dead, but also a place where the dead can be punished). Indeed, as Christian thought evolved, Hades became synonymous with hell.

The biblical scholar W.F. Albright states that the Hebrew root for Sheol is Shaal, which usually means 'to ask, to interrogate, to question.' Sheol therefore should mean 'asking, interrogation, questioning.' This is significant, as it would show that Sheol is the place where the 'soul' is questioned about, or 'judged' on, its earthly existence.

Ethical perspectives

If one considers that there is no such thing as an afterlife, how would that affect the religious believer in terms of behaviour in this life? The ideas of heaven/paradise in the Western religions seem to suggest that good behaviour will be rewarded in the afterlife. If this is not the case, then it would be a logical question to ask 'Why should I be good?' Likewise any fear of punishment for bad behaviour would be erased if it were to be shown that hell did not exist either.

This also applies to the concept of samsara: with no possibility of rebirth/reincarnation, how could the soul reach enlightenment? Indeed, perhaps the non-existence of samsara would imply the non-existence of the soul, so would this not undermine the very foundations of belief within Hinduism, and to a similar extent, Buddhism and Sikhism?

When euthanasia or suicide occurs, many religions believe that this affects what happens in the next life. St Thomas Aquinas stated categorically that all forms of suicide, whether assisted or not, are against the will of God and the purpose of human existence. His natural moral law outlined five primary precepts and suicide goes against three of those, namely: it is the complete antithesis of living; it harms others and works against an ordered society; God is the only one to take life – suicide would contravene that and is therefore going against the precept of 'worshipping God'.

Research tasks

1 Find out the views of the following in relation to euthanasia or suicide:

1. Kant

2. Aristotle

3. Utilitarianism

4. Situation Ethics

2 Research whether or not a belief in life after death is desirable/required/ upheld by any ethical theories. Evaluate whether such a belief strengthens or weakens the ethical theory.

Chapter 5

Belief in Life after Death: an Evaluation

When discussing the evidential claims for life after death, we need to bear in mind precisely what it is we're discussing. Whilst much of the material that follows is from a philosophical standpoint, it is relevant to all areas of the Religious Studies specification. The significance of this evidence for religion will be highlighted later in the chapter, but it is possible to relate the content that follows to all areas, bearing in mind each religion's specific beliefs about what happens to a person after death.

There are, broadly speaking, two main possibilities of survival after death: one relates to the survival of the self without a body and the second relates to an existence with a body (both of these ideas are associated with the concept of Dualism – see Chapter 2). Within these ideas we are following the pattern outlined in Brian Davies's *An Introduction to the Philosophy of Religion*, which you may like to read for more detail – it will certainly enhance your understanding of this complex area.

The first concept, that of survival after death without the body, is an extremely old one. It can be found in Plato's writings but clearly pre-dates him. Plato's character Socrates is asked how he should be buried: Socrates replies by implying that whatever happens to his body after his death is irrelevant, as he 'himself' will be distinct from it. Socrates clearly believes that his body is no more than a temporary shelter for his 'real self', that thing which makes him Socrates! Indeed, according to Plato, we human beings are souls; our souls exist before they have bodies and continue to exist after the bodies perish; and our souls between embodiments can directly perceive the Forms. It is these non-corporeal entities which are the form of our existence after death.

The second concept is that we do have, in some form, a bodily existence after death, although there is a no small measure of uncertainty as to precisely what form this after-life body will take. It clearly cannot be the exact same body that we possess in this lifetime –there is overwhelming evidence that our current bodies will rot and decay in this world, long after we have 'died'. So what sort of bodies are we talking about? The Christian belief, as found in the Nicene Creed, states 'And we look for the resurrection of the dead, and the life of the world to come', which suggests that the dead will be, in some form, 'raised'. As the fundamental Christian teaching is that, in order to be human in the fullest sense we must possess both body and soul, then it is a logical extension to suggest that it is this dual nature that Christians can expect in an after-life. Aquinas himself makes this very point:

The natural condition of the human soul is to be united with the body…therefore man's final happiness requires the soul to be again united to the body.

According to Davies this leads on to two philosophical questions about the nature of survival after death:

The first can be regarded as conceptual. It basically asks whether or not our two views of life after death are possible....the second question, however, moves from possibility to actuality. It asks whether it is reasonable to believe that we can look forward to disembodied survival or resurrection.

It may not be possible to find clear answer to these questions. The concept of 'eschatological verification' (a phrase coined by John Hick, referring to the idea that we will discover the truth about certain 'ultimate' questions after we die) is one which we might like to apply here. There are, however, claims to an existence after death and it is to these that we now turn our attention.

Research/writing tasks

Using magazines, newspapers and online articles you should:
- Collect a series of articles (between 5-10) relating to people talking about experiences that suggest there may be life after death i.e. Near Death Experiences, Mediums, etc.
- Write a brief account where you assess the reliability of the accounts that you have selected. You should note in your account any common features that the articles may have.

Claims of evidence for life after death

a) Near Death Experiences

The 'near-death experience' term was popularized by Raymond Moody's best-selling collection of accounts in 1975. Many similar accounts had been collected prior to this and can be found in literature across a whole variety of cultures. The basic features tend to be similar (including tunnels, lights, out-of-body journies and visions) but the specific content may vary.

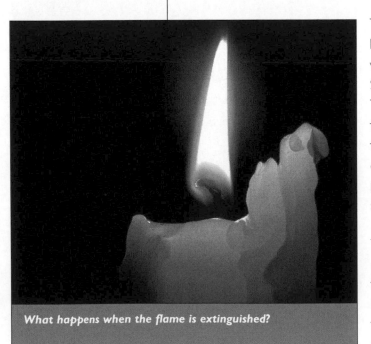
What happens when the flame is extinguished?

The characteristics of NDEs from Raymond Moody's book *Life After Life* (1975) can be found listed on the website of The International Association for Near-Death Studies inc. (web address: http://iands.org/index.php). This site gives clear details of the various types of NDE that have been documented, as well as descriptors of the stages common to NDEs. What then do these characteristics tell us? Do they give final and clinching proof in a life after death? Or are they open to suspicion and scepticism?

The sceptics certainly exist. Many consider the experiences to be no more than a kind of wishful thinking, or even a perceived reality altered through the use of drugs. However, this does not take into account the fact that these accounts transcend age and culture and this leads us to the question of why this should be?

Other scientific claims have posited theories to try to explain the phenomenon of NDEs. Amongst the suggestions are: lack of oxygen to the brain; the stimulation of receptors in nerve cell membranes, called NMDA receptors; the effects of the neurotransmitter serotonin; and even the level of endorphins (the brain's own morphine-like chemicals).

Experimentation has demonstrated that when the brain is given certain electrical stimulation, the subject can undergo a whole range of experiences, including floating, flying, flashbacks on life, tunnels, lights and spirals. Whilst these purely physiological explanations can cover many of the NDEs that are experienced, they cannot – currently – give sufficient evidence to prove that there is no such thing as life after death. Indeed, many would rather hope that the NDE was a 'sneak-peek' into the next world, rather than just the echoes of a dying brain!

b) Spiritualism

In his book *Philosophy of Religion*, John Hick states that the Spiritualist movement has long claimed that life after death has been verified beyond reasonable doubt by 'well-attested cases of communication between the living and the 'dead''. Spiritualism originated in the middle of the nineteenth century and became popular very quickly – so much so, that by the 1890s spiritualist séances were being held in major cities across Europe and America. In the most dramatic of these, mediums not only communicated messages from the dead, but generated 'physical phenomena' such as levitating tables, speech through trumpets, direct voices from the dead (i.e. without any trumpet or other instrument), and even full-body appearance of spirit forms.

Not surprisingly, the question of how the dead could influence the realm of the living was raised. A substance called ectoplasm, which was usually visible only to the naked eye (and to witnessing camera lenses) in darkness, was identified as the 'force' which caused these things to happen. There exist several photos of accomplished mediums producing the substance (a kind of white material) usually from their mouths. *The Oxford Companion to the Body* (2001), reports:

In the archives of the Society for Psychical Research in London, there is still a piece of Helen Duncan's [a famous medium] ectoplasm. This looks very much like a large piece of fine muslin and even has stitching around the edges. Although, like most other mediums, she was regularly searched before séances, many believe she swallowed and later regurgitated the material.

This scepticism, along with the advent of infra-red camera technology and the parallel diminishing of claims of ectoplasm production, seems to weaken the claims of spiritualism regarding the appearance of the dead in the land of the living. However, mediums and spiritualists have an entrenched position within Western society and remain popular today, despite such rejections from the scientific community.

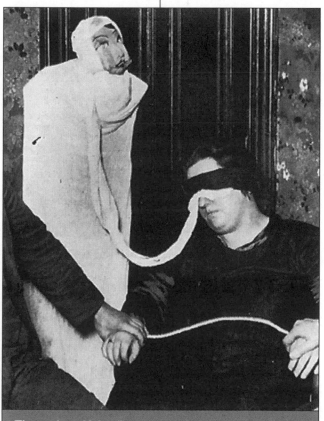

The medium Helen Duncan produces a materialised form of her spirit 'Peggy' at a séance in 1933

Discussion topic

How do the experiences of those claiming to have undergone a NDE relate to the idea of religious exclusivism? (i.e. no Christian is known to have seen Hindu gods, but neither is any Hindu known to have seen Jesus. Do you think that this is proof that NDEs are no more than personaal perceptions?

John Hick makes reference to the so called 'direct-voice medium' and to demonstrate that such mediums do not actually speak to the dead, he gives the following example:

a medium ... who produced the spirit of one 'Gordon Davies', who spoke in his own recognisable voice, displayed considerable knowledge about Gordon Davies, and remembered his death. This was extremely impressive until it was discovered that Gordon Davies was still alive; he was, of all ghostly occupations, a real-estate agent, and had been trying to sell a house at the time when the séance took place!

Nevertheless, the issue of whether or not the world of spiritualism makes any serious contribution to the matter of life after death is still under debate.

Research task

Using either the Library or the Internet, prepare a set of notes that argue the case both for and against Spiritualism as a means of communicating with the dead.

c) Alternative evidence

Those involved in psychological research have, over a number of years, collected a vast array of evidence to support the possibility of life after death. The findings from much of this research strongly suggest that the body and mind can exist independently of each other. Dr David Chalmers, in 1997, wrote in *Scientific American*:

Consciousness, the subjective experience of an inner self, could be a phenomenon forever beyond the reach of neuroscience. Even a detailed knowledge of the brain's inner workings ... may fail to explain how or why human beings have self-aware minds.

This would seem to suggest that there is something more, something intangible about human existence. Could this be a pointer towards the possibility that something of ourselves exists, and can keep on doing so, after our body has died?

It is possible to question why mankind has a spiritual nature. It is widely reported by anthropologists that, for every human civilization that has ever existed, there have always been signs of some kind of religious or spiritual dimension to their lives. Why should this be so?

Other claims involve out-of-body experiences (where an individual, either through voluntary meditative technique or involuntary reaction, has a sense of being separate from their material body, sometimes referred to as 'astral travelling'); ghostly apparitions (where a person perceives the physical presence of a non-corporeal entity, which seem to possess an individual intelligence and ability to move around a particular area); and claims of 'past life' awareness (where an individual may claim to have a recollection of having been alive before, usually many years ago, and can recall detailed events and places which suggest that they were present at that time in history). These all raise the question of what exactly is happening.

Added to this is the phenomenon of the child prodigy, where a young person displays talents beyond what is considered 'normal' for their age, thus prompting some to suggest that they have recollected the experiences of a previous incarnation and are still able to make use of skills previously learnt, despite being at such a young age. Are all such claims to be dismissed as false? Is it possible that such untested evidence can support a belief that there exists something beyond this mortal coil?

Research task

There have been many claims of 'psychic powers' such as telepathy, clairvoyance, precognition, dowsing, psychometry, xenoglossy, bi-location and psychokinesis. How might these claims be used to support a possible 'life after death' existence?
- Choose any three of the above and find out what they mean, how they work and what they suggest about the human mind.
- Explain whether you think they support the concept of Life after Death.

Writing task

What is meant by consciousness? Explain, with reference to the work of Dr David J. Chalmers.

d) Religious teaching

Evidence for the belief in life after death comes strongly from the religious traditions themselves. Within the sacred writings of the major world religions, an assertion that there is survival beyond this existence is unanimously made. (Refer to Chapter 4 for a more detailed explanation of each of these concepts).

Buddhist scripture indicates that it is only through constant rebirths and gaining the right karma that nirvana can eventually be achieved. Christianity teaches not only the resurrection of the body, but also that an eternity in God's presence is the reward for all the faithful. Hindu scriptures demonstrate that reincarnation is the fate of all living beings and that only by living correctly, through a series of lives, can the atman finally achieve Moksha. Islam promises paradise for the faithful Muslim, an eternity of bliss that is the just reward of the one who has lived life in perfect submission to the will of Allah. Judaism teaches of the reward for the just and punishment for the ungodly, and some Jews accept the possibility of reincarnation (although there are liberal Jews that deny the possibility of the afterlife). Finally, Sikhism looks forward to an eternity where the soul has become God-centered rather than self-centered.

Whilst all broadly agree on some kind of existence after death, it should be noted that the Western traditions tend to emphasise an individual existence after death, whereas the Eastern religions tend towards the concept of either reincarnation or being incorporated into a universal soul. Do these contradictions weaken belief in an afterlife? Or because both suggest an afterlife, but disagree as to what form it will take, is the case actually strengthened?

Discussion topic

Is the unanimity of religious teaching about an existence after death a strong reason for accepting life after death as fact?

Conclusion

The idea of life after death is one that is important to all religions. Whether that Life is a disembodied existence or whether it is embodied, we do not know for certain. Our various faith claims will lead us to one view over another. For the religious believer the significance of the existence of a life after death is intrinsic. The evidence for life after death remains widespread, yet confusing. But is that perhaps that is the way it should be? From the Old Testament comes the prohibition to consult mediums, not because they were fakes (see the account of Saul asking the medium at Endor to raise the spirit of Samuel), but rather because knowledge of what lies beyond this life is for God alone. Kant believed that logically speaking there must be a life after death (he referred to it as the 'immortality of the soul') simply because achieving the *summum bonum* (highest good) in this life was not possible for all. The teachings of all world religions point out the importance of acting well in this life and trusting that the next will be informed by what we do in the here and now. It is that trust, or faith, that lies at the heart of what it means to be a religious believer – to take what Kierkegaard calls 'the leap of faith'. Religious belief depends on this faith: the ability to 'prove' an existence after death is not important. What is important is obedience to the precepts of the religion and, in doing so, securing for ourselves the knowledge that we have lived a 'good life' before death.

Questions and Outline Answers

Question

(a) Explain some beliefs about the nature and purpose of human life.

(b) 'Religious beliefs about human life are not important for people today.'
Assess the validity of this statement.

Answer

This question requires you to demonstrate knowledge and understanding of beliefs about the nature and purpose of human life and be able to assess how significant such beliefs are in contemporary society.

Remember you must (until 2010) make use of material from at least two different areas of study in your answer.

(a) Relevant ideas include: humanity as Divinely created, as opposed to being the product of chance; mind/body debate (materialism, idealism, dualism;) concept of the soul and spirituality; need for identity and of community; human sin; sanctity of human life; free will/determinism; nature/nurture debate; concept of stewardship of the world; faith/reason debate; Aquinas' primary and secondary precepts and four cardinal virtues; preparation for after-life or further existence (in relation to resurrection, reincarnation, moksha, mukti, samsara, Sheol, judgement, eternal life).

(b) Assessment of the importance of religious beliefs about human life, with reference to at least two distinct areas of study. For example, you may argue that such beliefs have no relevance to non-believers, since they regard religion as having no rational basis, and little significance to some believers who are either more concerned about practical day-to-day living than theology or theories, or consider this life an ephemeral stage to a more significant existence etc. On the other hand, you may also argue that such beliefs are significant to many believers because they provide ethical motivation, help believers cope with suffering, give hope of eventual justice, promise reward for faith, give meaning to existence etc. Maximum of Level 3 for one-sided response.

Question

(a) Examine different religious ideas about life after death.

(b) 'The evidence for belief in life after death is so weak that the belief is just wishful thinking.' Evaluate this claim.

Answer

This question requires you to demonstrate knowledge and understanding of religious beliefs about life after death, and be able to assess the evidence on which such beliefs are based.

Remember you must (until 2010) make use of material from at least two different areas of study in your answer.

(a)   You will be expected to identify several different ideas and explain them for Levels 4 and 5 (e.g. resurrection, reincarnation, moksha, samsara, judgement, eternal life, sheol, etc.).

(b)   Evaluation of the strength of the basis for belief in life after death, with reference to at least two distinct areas of study (e.g. Philosophy of Religion and Buddhism). On the one hand, you should point to the universality of such belief, with examples of empirical evidence (e.g. memories of past lives, near-death experiences, mediumistic communication with the deceased and child prodigies), the logic of continuing existence for meaning in life etc. On the other hand, you should point to problems of evidence, psychological explanations of need for ultimate justice and meaning in life, and contradictory concepts between religions etc.
Maximum of Level 3 for one-sided response.

Question

> (a) Identify and explain some religious beliefs, teachings, writings or theories about the nature and purpose of human life.
> (b) Determine how important belief in life after death is in religion.

Answer

This question requires you to demonstrate knowledge and understanding of beliefs and views about the meaning of human life and be able to assess the importance of belief in life after death for a religious believer.
Remember you must (until 2010) make use of material from at least two different areas of study in your answer.

(a)   You will be expected to identify at least three different ideas and explain them for Levels 4 and 5 (e.g. divinely created, human sin, sanctity of human life, free will/determinism, resurrection, reincarnation, moksha, mukti, samsara, Sheol, judgement, eternal life).

(b)   Evaluation of the importance of belief in life after death in religion, with reference to at least two distinct areas of study. You should give consideration to at least three factors (e.g. ethical motivation, coping with suffering, hope of justice, reward for faith) for Levels 4 and 5. An answer which is confined to merely demonstrating the importance of life after death will not be given more than Level 3. You should consider whether this particular belief is central or peripheral to religion, integral or trivial. On the one hand, you may argue that belief in life after death has greater motivating impact than other beliefs and factors, because of its permanent/far-reaching consequences. On the other hand, you may argue that other beliefs and factors are of equal or greater influence as they are more tangible, basic, essential and have immediate impact.

Select Bibliography

Badham, P. and L. (1982) *Immortality or Extinction?* (Palgrave Macmillan) 0333259335

Davies, B. (2002) *An Introduction to the Philosophy of Religion* (OUP) [chapter 13] 0199263477

Fontana, D. (2005) *Is There an Afterlife?: A Comprehensive Overview of the Evidence* (O Books) 1903816904

Jordan, A. (2002) *Philosophy of Religion for A Level* (Nelson Thornes Ltd) [chapter 13] 0748767606

Moody, R. (1984) *Life after Life* (Bantam Books) 0553274848

Moody, R (2005) *The Light Beyond* (Rider & Co) 1844135802

Cooper, J. (2000) *Body, Soul and Life Everlasting* (Wm B Eerdmans Publishing Co) 0802846009

Segal, A.F. (2004) *Life After Death: A History of the Afterlife in Western Religion* (Doubleday Books) 0385422997

Singer, P. (1995) *Rethinking Life and Death: The Collapse of Our Traditional Ethics* (Saint Martin's Press) 0312118805

Webber, J. (1996) *Life After Death* (Abacus Educational Services) 1898653135

Articles on issues relating to the nature of life, death and life after death, exist in many general textbooks about religion and religious experiences.

Further information on these topics can also be found within many introductions to individual world religions and encyclopaedias of religion.